MW00387430

This book belongs to:

____

Long Bord

i Ponc

kinetic sand

~~GoFo~~ Crocs

Libby Pad

Klindic

Donuts

mony

Made in the USA
Monee, IL
11 May 2020

30681333R00066